American Indian Nations

The Pawnee

Farmers and Hunters of the Central Plains

by Karen Bush Gibson

Capstone press

Mankato, Minnesota

Capstone Press

1710 Roe Crest Drive, North Mankato, Minnesota 56003.
www.capstonepub.com

 Books published by Capstone Press are manufactured with paper
containing at least 10 percent post-consumer waste.

Library of Congress Cataloging-in-Publication Data
Gibson, Karen Bush.
    The Pawnee: Farmers and hunters of the central plains / by Karen Bush Gibson.
    p. cm.—(American Indian nations)
    Includes bibliographical references and index.
    ISBN-13: 978-0-7368-2181-0 (hardcover)   ISBN-10: 0-7368-2181-3 (hardcover)
    ISBN-13: 978-0-7368-4822-0 (paperback)   ISBN-10: 0-7368-4822-3 (paperback)
    1. Pawnee Indians—Juvenile literature. [1. Pawnee Indians. 2. Indians of North
America—Great Plains.] I. Title. II. Series.
E99.P3G53 2004
978.004'979—dc21   2002156009

Summary: Provides an overview of the past and present Pawnee people. Traces their
customs, family life, history, and culture, as well as relations with the U.S. government.

Editorial Credits
Charles Pederson, editor; Kia Adams, series designer; Molly Nei, book
designer and illustrator; Kelly Garvin, photo researcher; Karen Risch,
product planning editor

Photo Credits
Cover images: Pawnee home, Getty Images/Hulton Archive; Pawnee buffalo
robe, National Museum of the American Indian, Smithsonian Institution, photo
by Carmelo Guadagno

Art Resource/National Museum of American Art, Washington, D.C., 16;
Capstone Press/Gary Sundermeyer, 11; Corbis, 26; Corbis/Bettmann, 25;
Corbis/Burstein Collection, 13; Jim Argo, 4, 34, 40, 43; Kansas State Historical
Society, 8–9, 20, 22–23, 29, 36; Courtesy of Larry Echohawk, 39; Marilyn
"Angel" Wynn, 15, 44, 45; Newberry Library, 32–33; Pawnee County Historical
Society Museum, 30; Photo Disc Inc., 12; Courtesy of Smithsonian Institution
Libraries, Washington, D.C., 19; Stock Montage/The Newberry Library, 10

Capstone Press wishes to thank Annie Ross, Ph.D., of the University of
California-Davis Native American Studies Department for her assistance in
preparing this book.

Printed in the United States of America in North Mankato, Minnesota.
122011   006515R

Table of Contents

Features

Pawnee dancers gather together at powwows. The Pawnee work together to preserve their culture.

Chapter One

Who Are the Pawnee?

The Pawnee are a long-established American Indian nation. They have made their homes in the central and southern Great Plains of the United States for more than 700 years. The tribal homeland of the Pawnee is in the area now called Nebraska and parts of Kansas. The Pawnee were resourceful people who adjusted well to the plains' severe weather conditions. They became successful farmers and hunters.

The Pawnee Nation today is made up of four Native American nations. They are the Chaui (Grand), the Kitkihahki (Republican), the Petahauirata (Tappage), and the Skidi (Wolf) Pawnee. The Pawnee called themselves "chahiksichahiks," meaning "men of men."

The word "Pawnee" may come from Caddoan-language words that sound similar. In Caddoan, "pariki" means horn. Pawnee warriors used paint and buffalo fat to make their hair stand up like a horn. The Caddoan word "parisa" means hunter. The Pawnee were known as great hunters of the plains.

Today, the Pawnee live throughout the United States and all over the world. More than half of all Pawnee live on or near the tribe's land near the city of Pawnee, Oklahoma. According to the 2000 U.S. Census, 2,485 people identify themselves as members of the Pawnee Nation.

Today's Pawnee work in a variety of professions. They are doctors, lawyers, businesspeople, and professionals. Some Pawnee people work for the Pawnee Nation, located in Oklahoma.

The Pawnee are a deeply spiritual people. They draw strength from their beliefs and the natural world around them. They are committed to preserving their culture.

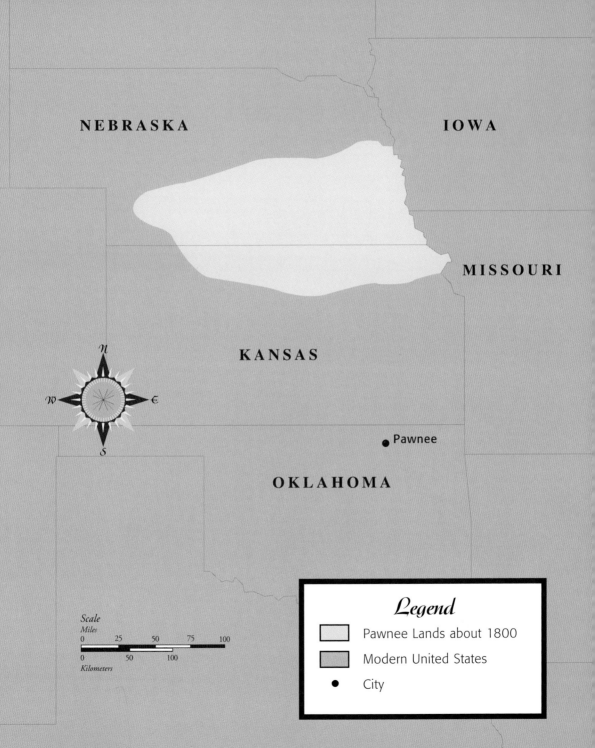

NEBRASKA

IOWA

MISSOURI

KANSAS

• Pawnee

OKLAHOMA

Scale
Miles
0   25   50   75   100
0   50   100
Kilometers

Legend

Pawnee Lands about 1800

Modern United States

• City

The Pawnee lived in Nebraska and parts of Kansas.

Chapter Two

Traditional Life

No one knows exactly when the Pawnee first came to the Great Plains. This region stretches from the Mississippi River west to the Rocky Mountains. By 1541, the Pawnee were settled in Nebraska and parts of Kansas.

The Pawnee obtained food by farming and hunting. They lived in villages along rivers. During the spring, the Pawnee planted their fields with corn, squash, beans, and pumpkins. When the plants were well established, the Pawnee left for a summer buffalo hunt.

On buffalo hunts, men hunted the animals. Women set up a camp and prepared the meat and hides. The Pawnee returned to their village in early autumn to harvest the crops. After the harvest, the people left for the year's second buffalo hunt.

Buffalo hunts were an important event for the Plains Indians.

Pawnee Corn and Squash

The Pawnee referred to corn as "the mother." They grew several varieties of corn, which they used in many dishes. This recipe pairs corn with squash, another vegetable the Pawnee grew. Ask an adult to help you cook the recipe below.

What You Need
Ingredients

1 medium onion
1 red bell pepper
1 medium squash with yellow flesh
2 tablespoons (30 mL) butter or corn oil
2 cups (480 mL) frozen whole kernel yellow sweet corn, thawed

½ cup (120 mL) parsley, finely chopped
¼ teaspoon (1.2 mL) salt
¼ teaspoon (1.2 mL) pepper
½ cup (120 mL) water or chicken broth
parsley for garnish, if desired

Equipment

kitchen knife
cutting board
measuring spoons
dry-ingredient measuring cups

liquid-ingredient measuring cup
large frying pan with lid
wooden mixing spoon

What You Do

1. Chop the onion and pepper.
2. Cut the squash into small cubes.
3. Warm butter or oil in large frying pan over medium heat.
4. Quickly fry onion for 3 to 5 minutes, stirring to cook evenly.
5. Add the squash and chopped pepper. Stir well, cover, and cook for 5 minutes.
6. Add corn and the remaining ingredients. Stir well, reduce heat, and cover. Cook for 10 to 15 minutes. Stir once or twice. Serve warm.

Makes 10 to 12 servings

Corn

Corn was an important food for the Pawnee. They often called it "the mother."

Corn planting began in the spring after the ground thawed. The Pawnee worked the soil with hoes made of buffalo bone and rakes of deer or antelope antlers. The best ears of corn from the previous year were soaked in fertilizer, then planted in the ground. These prepared seeds grew more quickly.

The Pawnee built platforms near the crops. The women and children sat on the platforms to guard the crops from birds and other animals.

At harvest time, most of the corn was dried and stored in buffalo skin pouches. These pouches were left in large pits in the ground and covered with branches. A hole was left in the branches so the people could take out corn as needed to eat. The remaining corn was saved for planting the following spring.

Villages

Villages focused on the good of everyone in the village. The people worked together and shared. A typical village had about a dozen earth homes called lodges. From a distance, they looked like small hills. Earth lodges were round like a dome. An average lodge was about 40 feet (12 meters) across the middle and 15 feet (4.6 meters) high.

The Pawnee lived in earth lodges. A Pawnee village often had about a dozen earth homes.

To make a lodge, the Pawnee set a frame of sturdy logs into the ground in a circle. Beams were placed on top of the logs for the roof. Willow branches lay on top of the beams. The framework was then covered with mud and grass. Holes in the top of the lodge allowed smoke from cooking fires to escape. Beds were located on the north and south sides of the earth lodge. The lodge's covered entrance faced the east, a symbol of spiritual knowledge.

Buffalo Hunt Camps

During buffalo hunts, the Pawnee used portable homes called tepees. Tepees were like tents that could be moved quickly. They were made of about 15 buffalo skins sewn together and stretched around a cone-shaped frame of straight poles.

When the buffalo herds moved, the Pawnee moved their hunting camp to follow them. The women took down the tepees. At the new camp, the women set up the tepees again.

The women used the tepee poles to make a sledlike travois. The Pawnee moved their belongings by piling them on this A-shaped frame. At first, the Pawnee used dogs to pull the travois. Around 1540, the Spanish introduced horses to the Pawnee. After that time, the Pawnee used horses to pull the travois. Horses were stronger than dogs and could carry much heavier loads and travel faster.

The Importance of Buffalo

The Pawnee used many parts of the buffalo they killed. They used the buffalo for food, clothes, and other purposes.

The Pawnee did not waste any part of the buffalo. Buffalo hides were often used as robes or blankets. The rawhide became leather to make clothes. Rawhide was sometimes used to make shields and drums. Horns and bones were used for tools and cups. Buffalo hair made good brushes, rope, and cushion stuffing. Buffalo manure made a good fuel for fires.

To thank the buffalo spirit for all it gave, the Pawnee performed a buffalo dance. Each dancer wore a buffalo head mask. A long piece of buffalo hide hung over the dancer's back. Dancers imitated buffalo movements while other people chanted and sang.

Horse Chief was a Grand Pawnee Head Chief. He and other Pawnee chiefs made decisions for their villages.

Family Life

Pawnee children lived mainly with their mother and grandparents. Grandmothers were often like a second mother. Grandfathers taught lessons to children through stories and games.

Pawnee children learned how to fit into the village in several ways. Pawnee girls watched their mothers and grandmothers work. Their mothers taught them to cook, sew, and garden. Young girls played with toy tepees and dolls. Young girls fed their brothers and sisters with food from their own garden plots.

Pawnee boys often left home around age 10 to live with an uncle. The uncle taught his nephew to ride horses, hunt, fight, and make tools and weapons. The uncle taught the boy to use spears to hunt quail and prairie chickens.

The men of the village had certain duties. As hunters, they were responsible for killing enough buffalo for their families to eat.

Men of the village served as chiefs and warriors. Chiefs listened to the other Pawnee before making decisions. Warriors fought to protect their people or their hunting grounds.

The lives of Pawnee women were busy. They took care of children and prepared meals. They were the heads of the households and the family farms. When it was time for a buffalo hunt, women packed and often carried the supplies from camp to camp.

Men killed the buffalo, but women had to prepare every part of the animal. Women made tepees, bowls, spoons, and tools from parts of buffalo. Women cooked the meat or dried it.

Marriage

Young men were considered ready for marriage by about age 18 and girls by about age 15. A man showed he wanted to marry a woman by giving gifts to her family. If the woman's family accepted the gifts, the village women held a ceremonial corn planting. The planting was a sign that the marriage would be a good one.

The Pawnee could have more than one spouse. Most often, men had more than one spouse. Often, a second wife was the sister of the first wife.

Spiritual Life

Religion has long been a part of the everyday life of the Pawnee. The Pawnee believed in several gods of the sky. A god named Tirawa was the chief god of all the spirits. The Pawnee

Pitalesharo (1797-1874)

The Pawnee practiced many religious ceremonies. They held ceremonies at the time of corn planting. The Pawnee sometimes held ceremonies in honor of the spirits, such as Morning Star. Some Pawnee believed that sacrificing a person's life to Morning Star would please the spirit and aid in the growth of their crops.

Pitalesharo, a Pawnee chief and warrior, did not agree with this practice. He encouraged members of his tribe to change their religious rituals. Pitalesharo soon gained followers who agreed with him. By 1838, the Pawnee no longer practiced this ceremony.

In addition to being a leader to his people, Pitalesharo was recognized by others. In 1821, Pitalesharo visited Washington, D.C., with a group of Indian leaders. During Pitalesharo's trip, American artist Charles Bird King painted his picture.

also believed that Tirawa created everything. The Pawnee believed that the stars were spirits. Morning Star, Evening Star, North Star, and South Star held up the four corners of the sky. Morning Star and Evening Star were the parents of the first humans, who were the Pawnee.

The Pawnee offered gifts of food, plants, and animals to different spirits. The Pawnee believed spirits lived in plants, animals, rocks, and even the weather.

The people joined dancing and ceremonial societies called Hedushka. The priests led important religious ceremonies for seasonal events like the harvest and buffalo hunts.

Groups of Pawnee gathered together for religious ceremonies.

Following the Stars

Archaeologists found a star chart of the night sky in a Pawnee sacred bundle. The star chart shows that the Pawnee paid close attention to the stars. The chart shows the Milky Way and many star patterns, called constellations, known today. The star chart is now at The Chicago Field Museum of Natural History.

The Pawnee made many decisions based on the position of the stars in the sky. The planting of crops depended on constellations. Earth lodges were built to line up with constellations at specific times of the year.

Honoring the sacred bundles was also important. These bundles held religious items, such as a pipe, tobacco, corn, and certain animal parts. The bundles were believed to be gifts from the stars. If the bundles were treated incorrectly, terrible things could happen to the Pawnee. Families and important individuals also had sacred bundles. The chief kept the village bundle. Women kept the family bundles. Sacred bundles were passed from parents to children. They were kept in a place of honor on the west side of the lodge.

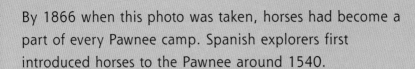

By 1866 when this photo was taken, horses had become a part of every Pawnee camp. Spanish explorers first introduced horses to the Pawnee around 1540.

Chapter Three

Change Comes to the Pawnee

For several hundred years after moving to the Great Plains, the Pawnee continued to live a traditional life. They planted and harvested their crops. They continued their star religion. They hunted buffalo twice a year.

In 1540, Spanish explorers introduced horses to the Pawnee and other American Indians. The introduction of horses changed the Pawnee way of life. The Pawnee could move farther and faster during buffalo hunts or battles with enemies.

In 1804, the Pawnee met the members of the Lewis and Clark Expedition. This group of American explorers was mapping the Missouri River on the orders of President Thomas Jefferson. The explorers wrote in their journals about meeting the Pawnee. The explorers moved on and did not stay with the Pawnee. At that time, about 10,000 Pawnee lived on the Great Plains.

In later years, meeting white settlers had tragic effects on the Pawnee. American travelers heading west carried cholera and smallpox germs. The Pawnee were unfamiliar with these diseases. Their bodies were not able to fight the germs. An 1831 smallpox outbreak killed more than half the Pawnee. An outbreak of cholera killed about 1,200 Pawnee in 1849.

Pressure to Change

Beginning in the 1830s, the United States government made treaties with the Pawnee. Each treaty took away more land from the Pawnee.

The 1857 Table Creek Treaty took all of the Pawnee land in exchange for a small reservation in Nebraska. The former Pawnee land was opened to American settlers. The U.S. government promised the Pawnee a sawmill, flour mill,

The Pawnee met with officials from the U.S. government to protect their land. Treaties were formed at this meeting.

The Pawnee Scouts

During the 1860s, the Lakota Sioux had many conflicts with settlers entering their land. The U.S. government had promised to keep settlers off Lakota land. But the settlers continued to enter the land. As a result, the Lakota decided to drive the settlers away with attacks.

In 1865, U.S. Army Major Frank North hired Pawnee men as army scouts to help stop the Lakota attacks. The Pawnee agreed to help the army find the camps of their traditional enemies. The army pay helped support hungry Pawnee families.

In 1868, Pawnee scouts helped protect workers building the first railroad across the plains. Cheyenne, Arapaho, and Lakota warriors had attacked the workers several times. With the Pawnee scouts' help, the workers completed the railroad in 1869.

After 1877, the army no longer used Pawnee scouts, but the Pawnee continued to serve in the armed forces. They fought in the Spanish-American War (1898). They also served in World War I (1914–1918), World War II (1939–1945), the Korean War (1950–1953), the Vietnam War (1954–1975), and the Gulf War (1991).

blacksmith shop, schools, and stores. These buildings were of little use to the Pawnee.

In the following years, settlers made more demands of the Pawnee. Settlers demanded that the Pawnee give up their traditional ways of life. The U.S. government listened to the settlers' demands. Government officials told the Pawnee to farm like the settlers. The Pawnee gave up their earth lodges and lived in wood-frame houses.

Religious missionaries arrived to teach the Pawnee about Christianity. This religion follows the life and teachings of Jesus Christ. Missionaries pressured the Pawnee to give up more of their customs and religious practices.

Worsening Conditions

Over the years, conditions worsened for the Pawnee. Crops failed because of droughts. Grasshoppers came and killed even more crops. Settlers sometimes attacked the Pawnee. They believed the Pawnee were responsible for attacks made by other Plains Indians.

Although the Pawnee helped with the building of the railroad, the railroad created new problems for them. In the 1860s and 1870s, trains carried buffalo hunters to the plains. The hunters killed hundreds of buffalo at a time. They left the meat of the buffalo to rot. At the same time, the Pawnee and other Plains Indian nations went hungry because they could not find enough buffalo for their own use.

Relationships with Nebraska settlers continued causing problems for the Pawnee. Settlers did not like seeing the Pawnee in town. Settlers also wanted Pawnee reservation land. They wanted the trees for building and the land for their cattle.

The Pawnee call their last five years in Nebraska the frightful years. Settlers demanded that the Pawnee be removed from reservation land. Swarms of grasshoppers ate the crops of both the settlers and Pawnee. The U.S. government helped the settlers but not the Pawnee.

In 1873, the Pawnee made their last big buffalo hunt. They were hunting near the Republican River in Nebraska. A force of about 1,000 Lakota Sioux warriors attacked the Pawnee hunting party. The Lakota killed several hundred Pawnee. Finally, the Pawnee had no choice but to leave for Indian Territory, now called Oklahoma. During 1874 and 1875, the U.S. government placed the Pawnee on

The Pawnee lived in tepees made from buffalo skins.

Moses YellowHorse (1898-1964)

Moses YellowHorse was the first man of completely American Indian background to play major league baseball. YellowHorse was a Pawnee born in Pawnee, Oklahoma, in 1898. Like many Pawnee children of that time, he attended boarding school. During the boys' free time, they played baseball. YellowHorse was an excellent baseball player.

In 1921, YellowHorse became a professional pitcher for the Pittsburgh Pirates. He pitched well for two seasons. In 1923, he moved to the minor leagues due to arm trouble. His baseball career ended in 1926.

After his baseball career, YellowHorse returned to Pawnee, Oklahoma. There, he worked at several different jobs. The people of Pawnee remember YellowHorse as a kind man and a leader of the Pawnee. YellowHorse died in 1964. The Pawnee honor YellowHorse with the Moses YellowHorse Softball Tournament at their Homecoming Festival held each July in Pawnee, Oklahoma.

390,000 acres (158,000 hectares) of land in northern
Indian Territory, west of the Arkansas River. The Pawnee
left Nebraska before harvesting their crops. They arrived in
Indian Territory in June. That was too late to plant new
crops. Without food, many Pawnee died from hunger and
disease. By 1876, about 2,000 Pawnee were left.

More Laws

The General Allotment Act of 1887 gave each head of an
American Indian family in the United States 160 acres
(65 hectares) of land. After the head of each Pawnee family
received land, about 230,000 acres (93,000 hectares) were
left. The U.S. government sold or gave this land to settlers.

In 1898, the Curtis Act forced American Indians to live
more like settlers did. This act outlawed tribal governments.
Indians could no longer speak their own languages, dress in
traditional clothes, or practice their religions.

Beginning around 1900, many American Indian children
were placed in boarding schools. One purpose of these
live-in schools was to make the children fit in better with

American culture. At the schools, Pawnee children lived far from their families and villages. They could speak only English and had to dress like settlers. They could not practice their traditions or ceremonies. They did not see their families for long periods of time. The boarding school period continued for many years.

Finally, the Pawnee regained control from the U.S. government. In 1934, the Wheeler-Howard Act allowed the Pawnee to reorganize and have their own government. In 1957, the Pawnee were allowed to use unsold Pawnee reservation land. In 1968, the original 390,000 acres (158,000 hectares) of Oklahoma reservation land were returned to Pawnee control. The Pawnee still control the land today.

Many Pawnee children were placed in boarding schools,
where they had to wear American-style clothes.

Along with its own government, the Pawnee tribe has its own police force.

Chapter Four

The Pawnee Today

Pawnee, Oklahoma, is the center of Pawnee life today. Many Pawnee people live in or near this town in northern Oklahoma, northeast of Oklahoma City. The central government of the Pawnee Nation is located here.

The government of the Pawnee Nation has two councils, each with eight people. The Business Council represents the entire Pawnee Nation. The council manages day-to-day Pawnee affairs. The chiefs' council, or Nasharo Council, is made up of two members from each of the four

Pawnee nations. The Nasharo Council deals with matters related to treaties or tribal membership.

The Pawnee government has similarities to the U.S. government. A constitution explains their laws. A bill of rights guarantees freedom of worship, freedom of speech, and other rights. A judicial system provides courts to make certain that laws are followed.

Members of the Pawnee Business Council represent the Pawnee Nation.

The Pawnee Nation sponsors many programs to help its people. Committees oversee the health, educational, and economic needs of the Pawnee. The Pawnee are building a Pawnee Indian Health Center, scheduled to open in 2004. The nation provides money to students who want to attend schools. The nation also helps Pawnee find jobs and receive job training.

Tribal Flag

The Pawnee Nation adopted a tribal flag in 1977. It features a blue background with a red wolf's head, symbolizing courage. A pipe and tomahawk are crossed beneath the wolf. They stand for peace and war. An American flag is above the wolf's head. It represents friendship with the United States. Four eagle feathers attached at the top of the flag represent the four Pawnee nations. Seven arrowheads at the bottom of the flag represent wars in which the Pawnee have fought. These wars include Indian wars, the Spanish-American War, World War I, World War II, the Korean War, the Vietnam War, and the Gulf War.

Education

Around 1900, a boarding school was built in Pawnee, Oklahoma. The school was called Pawnee Industrial School. Its nickname was Gravy U because its kitchen served gravy at many meals. Students at the school learned to farm or take care of dairy cattle. The school closed in 1958. The land was returned to the Pawnee nation in 1968.

Today, education is important to the Pawnee. Pawnee children attend public schools in and around Pawnee, Oklahoma. In these schools, teaching Pawnee culture is part of the learning plan. Some Pawnee attend language classes to learn their language. The Pawnee Nation provides scholarships to Pawnee who want to attend college.

Religion

Many modern Pawnee belong to the Native American Church. This religion blends traditional native beliefs with Christianity. The Native American Church has about 250,000 members. Indians from many nations belong to the religion. It is the largest American Indian religion in the United States, with churches in 24 states and Canada. The Pawnee attend services in the Pawnee community building, located in Pawnee, Oklahoma.

Larry Echohawk (1949-)

One of the best-known American Indian politicians in the late 1900s is Larry Echohawk. Born in 1949 in Wyoming, Echohawk had a Pawnee mother and a German father. Echohawk is one of six children.

Echohawk served in the U.S. Marine Corps and then earned a bachelor's degree from Brigham Young University in 1970. He earned a law degree from the University of Utah in 1973. After that, he worked for California Indian Legal Services. This organization offers legal help to American Indians.

In 1980, Echohawk moved to Idaho. In 1991, he became the first American Indian elected as Idaho's attorney general. He served on the Idaho Commission for Children and Youth.

Echohawk was twice elected to the Idaho House of Representatives. He chaired the Idaho delegation to the 1992 Democratic National Convention. He was the first American Indian to lead a state group to the convention. Among the honors he has received are the Martin Luther King medal for human rights and Children's Advocate of the Year. Today, Echohawk is a law professor at Brigham Young Law School.

The Pawnee continue to honor their culture
with powwows.

Chapter Five

Sharing Pawnee Traditions

The Pawnee work hard to preserve their culture. One way they do this is through festivals and ceremonies. The best-known celebration is the Homecoming Festival. This gathering takes place each July in Pawnee, Oklahoma. Created to honor Pawnee military veterans, the celebration has one of the oldest and largest powwows in the United States.

Music and dance are important parts of Pawnee powwows. Pawnee men sit at a large drum and play while both men and women sing. Some songs tell Pawnee history and help the Pawnee remember their old ways. Many Pawnee enjoy dancing at these powwows.

The circle is a common shape in Pawnee culture. Many Pawnee powwows and ceremonies are held within circles. Pawnee earth lodges are circular. They continue to be used for special events. Since the 1970s, many Pawnee ceremonies and meetings have been held in the Pawnee Roundhouse. This community center is built in the shape of a traditional earth lodge.

The Pawnee continue their culture with special projects. Some of these projects include an elder center and youth center. By meeting the needs of today's young and old Pawnee, the Pawnee Nation hopes to continue the nation's culture. The Pawnee actively seek the return of Pawnee items from museums, governments, and private citizens.

The Pawnee also aim to protect their culture through teaching their language. The Pawnee Nation's Education Department has provided Pawnee language classes since 1992. Learning materials for teaching the Pawnee language are currently being updated.

Sharing Pawnee traditions among themselves and with other people keeps the Pawnee culture alive. Dancing, music, language, and celebrations are all ways the Pawnee show they are proud of who they are. They believe their pride will carry them far into the future.

Teachers provide language classes for the Pawnee. The Pawnee work to keep their language and culture alive.

Pawnee Timeline

More than half the
Pawnee die during
a smallpox outbreak.

Major Frank North
organizes the Pawnee
scouts to help the
U.S. Army against
the Lakota Sioux.

1541 **1831** **1857** **1865** **1874–1875**

The Pawnee are
settled in Nebraska
and parts of Kansas.

After signing the Table
Creek Treaty, the Pawnee
move onto a small
reservation in Nebraska.

The Pawnee leave
Nebraska for
Indian Territory.

Saddle bag

Pawnee drum

The General Allotment Act passes, dividing reservation land into small plots for individual families.

The Pawnee flag is adopted.

1887   **1968**   **1977**   **2004**

The Pawnee Indian Health Center opens.

The U.S. government returns ownership of original reservation land to the Pawnee Nation.

Glossary

ceremony (SER-uh-moh-nee)—traditional words, music, or actions used to celebrate a special occasion

lodge (LODJ)—a Pawnee home

powwow (POU-wou)—a social and spiritual celebration of American Indian people that includes dancing

tepee (TEE-pee)—a cone-shaped tent made of buffalo skins and long poles

travois (truh-VOI)—a simple vehicle made of two trailing poles and a platform or net to carry a load

Internet Sites

Do you want to find out more about the Pawnee?
Let FactHound, our fact-finding hound dog, do the research for you.

Here's how:

1) Visit *www.facthound.com*
2) Type in the **Book ID** number:
   0736821813
3) Click on **FETCH IT**.

FactHound will fetch Internet sites picked by our editors just for you!

Places to Write and Visit

Oklahoma Historical Society
2100 North Lincoln Boulevard
Oklahoma City, OK 73105

Pawnee Indian Village State Historical Site
Kansas State Historical Society
480 Pawnee Trail
Republic, KS 66964-9618

The Pawnee Nation of Oklahoma
P.O. Box 470
Pawnee, OK 74058

For Further Reading

Gray-Kanatiiosh, Barbara A. *The Pawnee.* Native Americans. Edina, Minn.: Abdo Publishers, 2002.

Kallen, Stuart A. *The Pawnee.* Indigenous Peoples of North America. San Diego: Lucent Books, 2001.

Sita, Lisa. *Indians of the Great Plains: Traditions, History, Legends, and Life.* Native Americans. Milwaukee: Gareth Stevens, 2000.

Index